Comptroller of the Currency
Administrator of National Banks

Duties and Responsibilities of Directors

Comptroller's Handbook
(Section 501)

Narrative - March 1990, Procedures - January 1998

Management

Duties and Responsibilities of Directors (Section 501)

Table of Contents

Directors are placed in positions of trust by the bank's shareholders, and both statute and common law place responsibility for the management of a bank firmly and squarely on the board of directors. The directors of a national bank may delegate the day-to-day routine of conducting the bank's business to their officers and employees, but they cannot delegate their responsibility for the consequences of unsound or imprudent policies and practices whether it involves lending, investing, protecting against internal fraud, or any other banking activity. The directorate is responsible to its depositors and shareholders for safeguarding their interests through the lawful, informed, efficient, and able administration of the institution.

The affairs of each national banking association are to be managed by directors who, initially, are elected by the shareholders at a meeting held before the association is finally authorized to commence business and afterward, at meetings to be held, at least annually, on a day specified in the bylaws. The directors hold office for 1 year and until their successors are elected and have qualified. The number of directors of each national association is limited to not less than five, nor more than 25. Various laws govern the election, required number, qualifications, oath, liability, and removal of directors or officers, as well as disclosure requirements for outside business interests. Other laws pertain to certain restrictions, prohibitions, and penalties relating to securities dealers as directors, officers, or employees, interlocking directorates, purchases from directors and sales to directors, commissions and gifts for procuring loans, embezzlement, abstraction, willful misapplication, false entries, and penalty for political contributions, and other matters. The examiner must be familiar with these laws and the related regulations and interpretative rulings.

A record of supervisory actions by directors is to be kept, as specified by the bylaws, in a directors' meeting minute book.

Directors' Responsibilities

An examiner sometimes has to impress bank directors with the extent of his or her duties and responsibilities. Unless bank directors realize the importance of their positions and act accordingly, they are failing to discharge their obligations to the shareholders and depositors. They are also failing to take advantage of the opportunity to exercise a sound and beneficial influence on the economy of their community. The following are the major responsibilities of bank directors:

- To select competent executive officers—It is a primary duty of a board of directors to select and appoint executive officers who are qualified to administer the bank's affairs effectively and soundly. It is also the responsibility of the board to dispense with services of officers who prove unable to meet reasonable standards of executive ability and efficiency.

- To effectively supervise the bank's affairs—The charter and degree of supervision required of a bank's board of directors to assure a soundly managed bank involves reasonable business judgment and competence, and sufficient time to become informed about the bank's affairs. Directors cannot avoid responsibility for their bank's sound management or its problems. If supervisory negligence is involved, a director's responsibility may extend to personal financial responsibility. The responsibility of directors to supervise the bank's affairs may not be delegated to the active executive officers. Directors may delegate certain authority to executive officers but not the primary responsibility to maintain the bank and its policies on a sound and legal basis.

- To adopt and follow sound policies and objectives—The directors must provide a clear framework of objectives and policies within which the chief executive officer must operate and administer the bank's affairs. Such objectives and policies should cover all areas. Some of the more important areas would be investments, loans, asset and liability management, profit planning and budgeting, capital planning, and personnel policies. The examination of such policies is covered in other sections of this handbook.

- To avoid self-serving practices—A self-serving board, whether weak or strong in other respects, is a dangerous board. The fact that individuals are bank directors does not increase their borrowing privileges, it simply increases their borrowing responsibilities. A bank's directors bear a greater-than-normal responsibility in dealing with the loans to members of the directorate. They must make decisions that preclude the possibility of partiality or favored treatment. Unwarranted loans to a bank's directors or to their interests are a serious matter from the standpoint of credit and management. Losses that develop from such unwarranted loans are bad enough, but the weakening effect on the bank's general credit standards is likely to be even worse. Directors who become financially dependent on their bank normally lose their usefulness as directors. Other self-serving practices to which the examiner should be alert are:

– Gratuities to directors for the purpose of obtaining their approval of financing arrangements or the use of particular services.

– The use of bank monies by directors, officers, or shareholders to obtain loans or transact other business. Directors should be especially critical of correspondent bank balances when officers, directors, or shareholders are borrowing from the depository bank. The Department of Justice is of the opinion that certain interbank deposits connected with a loan to officers, directors, or shareholders of the depositing bank might constitute a misapplication of funds in violation of 18 USC 656.

– Transactions involving conflicts of interest. These always represent potentially self-serving transactions. When board decisions involving a potential conflict of interest are made, the director should fully disclose the manner in which the transaction tends to be beneficial and should abstain from voting on the matter. The abstention should be recorded in the minutes. The examiner should also be aware that sometimes ethical conflicts of interest can arise when a director, or director-related firm, performs professional services for the bank. For example, a director who is also the bank's legal counsel may not, in some situations, be able to advise or represent the bank in an objective manner.

• To be informed of the bank's condition and management policies—As part of a director's responsibility to be informed of the bank's condition and management policies, the OCC requires that all national banks, under a provision in their bylaws, provide for a director's examination.

When the directors lack adequate knowledge of examination techniques and procedures, they are encouraged to employ outside auditors to make some or all of the examination on their behalf. Such an examination, performed by an outside firm, is much more beneficial to the directors if the examining committee or the entire board plays an active role in it. Directors should participate at least to the extent of appraising policies, obtaining an understanding of the procedures to be employed by the auditor, and reviewing the audit report with the auditors. Before concluding the review, directors should understand thoroughly the significance of all of the details contained in the report. When outside auditing firms are utilized, the scope of the examination should include direct confirmation of a representative number of the bank's loans and deposits.

Whether the directors perform the examination or employ internal/external auditors, they must ensure that an adequate scope is established. The Internal and External Audits section (Section 102) of this handbook sets forth general criteria considered by examiners in determining if the bank's audit program is acceptable. Directors should review that section for guidance on setting an adequate scope for a director's examination.

Copies of the director's examination report and the reports by outside auditors should be retained in the bank's files and should be made available to examiners. When an accounting firm supplements its audit report with a letter report containing recommendations for improvements in internal controls, accounting, or other matters, the examiner should obtain a copy of it and should review its contents. Any significant deficiencies noted in the letter should be discussed with management to obtain correction.

- To maintain reasonable capitalization—A board of directors has the responsibility of maintaining its bank on a well- capitalized basis. A discussion of capital planning and capital adequacy is included in "Capital Accounts," and the examiner should be familiar with the information contained therein.

- To observe banking laws, rulings, and regulations—Directors must exercise care to see that banking laws are not violated. That duty may involve a financial responsibility for losses arising out of illegal actions.

- To ensure that the bank has a beneficial influence on the economy of its community—One reason for approving bank charters is to meet a specific community need. Directors, therefore, have a continuing responsibility to the community to provide those banking services that will be conducive to well-balanced economic growth. Directors should be certain that they attempt to satisfy all legitimate credit needs of the community. This is especially true for legitimate new and developing business credit. The examiner also should be familiar with the sections of this handbook dealing with future prospects and service area analysis.

Compliance with Formal and Informal Administrative Actions

Bank directors must ensure that management corrects deficiencies found in the bank. Instructions to do so may come from the OCC in the form of a formal or informal administrative action, depending on the severity of the problem.

Authority for a formal action is granted by the Financial Institutions Supervisory Act of 1966 (12 USC 1818). Formal actions, cease and desist orders, and agreements are normally exercised when banks have serious problems. For less serious problems, the OCC issues a "Memorandum of Understanding" or requests the bank to sign a commitment letter. Both of these actions are informal; the memorandum is an agreement between the District Deputy Comptroller and the bank setting forth required corrective action, whereas the commitment letter is a document signed only by the bank.

The Senior Deputy Comptrollers for Bank Supervision have the primary responsibility to use OCC's administrative authorities to accomplish the supervisory objectives.

The authority to initiate, negotiate, execute, modify, and terminate enforcement actions involving banks that are being supervised by the districts under PPM 5310-2 is delegated to the District Deputy Comptrollers or to the Deputy Comptroller for Special Supervision, if Special Supervision is involved in the supervision of those banks (see PPM 5310-3 for further details).

District personnel must monitor compliance with both types of administrative actions. To assist in that process, the district office and/or the portfolio manager are often provided with periodic progress reports by the bank. In addition, information is provided by the examiner-in-charge who will check compliance with the action during most on-site visits. All assessments of compliance should be documented in the Supervisory Monitoring System (SMS), and, when a report of supervisory activity (ROSA) is prepared, comments on the overall degree of compliance and what actions should be taken to maintain/obtain compliance should be made in the ROSA. Both SMS and ROSA comments should specify which articles are in compliance and which are not. In addition, comments on the effectiveness of the action, including whether additional administrative action should be taken, terminated, or modified should be made in SMS.

Depository Institution Management Interlocks Act

Under Title II of the Financial Institutions Regulatory and Interest Rate Control Act of 1978, interlocking relationships of management officials of various nonaffiliated depository institutions are prohibited, depending upon the asset size and geographical proximity of the organizations.

The intent of the act is to foster competition among various depository institutions by prohibiting interlocking management official relationships. However, four exceptions are permitted based on the public benefit that is derived from the interlocking relationship and on the competitive nature of the institutions involved. The exceptions are for:

- Institutions located in low-income areas or that are controlled or managed by members of a minority group or by women.

- Newly chartered institutions.

- Institutions in deteriorating condition.

- Institutions sponsoring a credit union.

Those exceptions are permissible only with prior OCC approval.

Interlocking relationships existing prior to November 10, 1978, and not in violation of 15 USC 19, are permitted to continue for a period of 10 years. Enforcement of the interlock provisions of the act carry full cease-and-desist powers.

General Procedures

Many of the steps in these examination procedures require gathering information from or reviewing information with examiners in others areas. Since other areas may include examination procedures that address duties and responsibilities of directors, discussing your review with them can reduce burden on the bank and avoid duplication of effort. Sharing examination data also can be an effective cross check of compliance and help examiners assess the integrity of management information systems.

Information from other areas should be appropriately cross-referenced in working papers. Information that is not available from other examiners should be requested directly from the bank.

Objective: To set the scope for review of duties and responsibilities of directors.

1. Obtain and review the following documents to identify items that require follow-up:

    ☐ Prior Report of Examination and related management and board responses.
    ☐ Internal/External audit reports.
    ☐ Bank policies regarding the board of directors (i.e., Insider policies).
    ☐ Correspondence between the bank and the OCC.

2. Determine any material changes in the composition of the board since the previous examination. Obtain or update the following:

    ☐ A list of directors to include:
    – Home address (if the director was appointed or elected since the previous examination, indicate the number of years residing at present address).
    – Date of birth.
    – Years as a director of the bank.
    – Approximate net worth.

          − Occupation.
          − If the director is an indenture trustee.
          − Citizenship.
          − Common stock ownership (beneficial, direct and indirect).
          − Bonus, fees, etc.

3.   Obtain a complete set of reports furnished to directors at the last board meeting and list the areas of operation covered by the reports. Ensure that these reports are representative of what they receive each meeting.

4.   Distribute copies of the reports furnished directors to examiners assigned other areas. Ask them to determine if reports are:

    • Prepared accurately;
    • Contain sufficient detail for decision-making; and
    • Submitted to the directors in a timely manner.

5.   Distribute a list of the insiders (executive officers, directors, and principal shareholders and their interests) to the appropriate examining personnel to ascertain the extent of loans to or transactions with insiders. Those examiners should be alert for any relationship with insiders that are not included on the list.

6.   Based on the performance of the previous steps and discussions with the bank EIC, determine the scope and set the objectives for this examination.

Quantity of Risk

Conclusion: The quantity of risk is (low, moderate, high)

Overall Board Responsibilities

Objective: To determine that the board is fulfilling its responsibility to effectively supervise the affairs of the bank.

1. Arrange with EIC or other examiner(s) assigned Management Appraisal to attend and participate in an introductory meeting with the President, CEO, Chairman, or other directors to obtain an overview of the bank from the board of director's perspective. Consider discussing:

    - The bank's current priorities and how strategic directives are set.
    - The bank's environment (business environment, regulatory and legal framework) including significant opportunities and challenges.
    - Current financial performance and how the board oversees it.
    - Efforts to select and retain capable management.
    - The adequacy of control systems given current and planned bank operations.
    - Progress in addressing deficiencies noted internally or by OCC, external auditors, etc.
    - Efforts to serve community credit needs.

2. Review reports furnished to directors and determine if they assist the board in meeting its responsibilities. Note types of reports the board does not receive for future discussion with EIC. As guidelines, consider the following:

    - A report on any major bank endeavor upon which each bank director is expected to make a decision. Examples include branch applications, major building plans, and the introduction of any new product or service.

    - Updates to strategic objectives, business plan, budget, etc.

    - An annual projection of the bank's capital needs.

- A full report of all new executive officer borrowings at any bank.

- A status report on litigation, including potential exposure. Also include any known pending or threatened litigation and potential exposure.

- All correspondence addressed to the board of directors from the OCC and any other significant correspondence.

- A monthly statement of condition or balance sheet and a monthly statement of income. Those statements should be in reasonable detail, and compared to the prior month, the same month of a prior year and to the budget. The directors should receive explanations for all large variances.

- Monthly statements of changes in all capital and reserve accounts. Such statements should explain any changes.

- Loan reports that list past due loans (at least 30 days), nonaccrual loans, trends in delinquencies, rate reductions, troubled debt restructures, other real estate owned, and large new loans granted since the last report.

- Investment reports that:
    - Segregate the portfolio into "available for sale", "hold to maturity", and "trading";
    - Group the securities by classifications;
    - Reflect the book value, market value, yield; and
    - Summarize purchases and sales.

- Interest rate risk reports reflecting the bank's on and off balance sheet activities.

- Information on borrowing by the bank, including the type, amount, frequency, duration, and rate as well as management's rationale.

- A monthly analysis of the bank's liquidity needs (i.e., sources and uses report).

- Audit and examination reports and responses to deficiencies.

- An annual presentation of bank insurance coverage

- An annual presentation on the bank's technology budget as well as system capacity during peak usage (i.e., ATMs, LAN).

- An annual presentation on the bank's contingency plan for continuing and resuming operations in the event of a disaster.

- Information about the local and national economy and their impact on the bank.

3. Read and brief the minutes of all meetings of the board since the last examination. Note the following:

    - Any actions taken in contravention of the by-laws.

    - Actions taken by the board which are not a part of a normal monthly meeting.

    - Resolutions or discussions about entrance into a new geographic area, customer service, asset or liability category, or other new undertaking. This should also include a discussion of updates to the strategic plan and how any new activities fit in with the plan.

    - Creation of any special committee and its mission.

    - Ratification by the full board of actions taken by standing committees.

    - If the minutes specify any transactions with directors or their interests, abstention of any interested director. If the minutes do not mention any director-related transactions that are uncovered during the examination, determine why it was not discussed during a board meeting. Also determine how it was approved and that the interested party refrained from voting.

- Directors who do not regularly attend meetings to determine the level of interest, dedication, and how they will fulfill fiduciary responsibilities.

- Participation of individual directors to determine if any one, or a certain group of directors, dominates the board discussions.

- Re-booked charged off loans approved by the board and the rationale for re-booking. Distribute list to examiner assigned Loan Portfolio Management.

- Reviews of correspondence between the OCC and the bank.

- Reports of examinations and audits reviewed and actions taken or plans to affect correction of deficiencies.

4. Aggregate violations of laws or regulations concerning directors that were disclosed in other areas of examination. Specifically review any violations discovered in " Insider Activities." Also discuss findings with examiners assigned other areas.

Specific Board Responsibilities and Activities

Select additional optional procedures given the findings from above.

Objective: To determine whether the directors have accepted their responsibility for selecting and retaining competent management.

1. Determine whether the board or a committee thereof reviews the chief executive officer's performance at least annually. If so, review the criteria considered for reasonableness.

    Evaluation criteria may include:

    - The bank's record of compliance with laws and regulations.
    - Criticisms contained in audit and examination reports, and their resolution.
    - Management's responsiveness to board directives, including compliance with board-approved policies.
    - The timeliness, quality, and accuracy of management's recommendations

and reports.
- Management's presentations to the board.

2. Determine whether the board or a committee thereof ensures that the performance of key management members is reviewed at least annually. If so, coordinate the review of the criteria used with the EIC and the examiner assigned Management Appraisal.

3. Discuss planned changes to management positions with EIC and appropriate bank officials. Determine rationale for changes.

4. If vacancies exist in senior level management positions, determine if, when, and how the vacancies will be filled. Also determine the board's criteria to fill those vacancies.

5. Obtain a copy of any management contracts. Brief the pertinent points, and determine reasonableness of terms.

6. Determine how the compensation of executive officers is set and who makes decisions concerning executive salaries. (12 CFR 30)

7. Note any titled individual who, by action of the board or by the by-laws, is specifically excluded from being an executive officer. (12 CFR 215.2(e)) Be alert for any policy-making decisions made by any titled officer specifically excluded from being an executive officer.

Objective: To determine whether the board's organizational structure provides it with adequate support.

1. Read and brief the minutes of the board's annual organization meeting and list standing committees and their members. Some examples of committees a bank may have depending on its size, scope of operations, risk profile, and board composition include:

    - Executive Committee
    - Audit Committee (Required for banks with assets over $500 million)
    - Fiduciary Audit Committee (Required if trust powers active)
    - Loan Committee
    - Asset/Liability Management Committee
    - Risk Management Committee

- Fiduciary Committee
- Compensation Committee
- Nominating Committee

2. Request that examiners read and brief the minutes of the standing committees as well as ad hoc committees in their assigned areas, specifically noting whether each committee's mission, authority, and responsibility are clear.

3. Prepare a list of major areas of operation that are not monitored by specific committees and determine the mechanism used for communicating information to the board.

4. Review the list of directors to determine if the board is comprised of individuals with different backgrounds and expertise.

Objective: To determine whether the board has accepted its responsibility to monitor operations.

Refer to Processes and Controls sections in Quality of Risk Management.

Objective: To determine whether the board has accepted its responsibility to oversee business performance.

1. Determine whether the board is knowledgeable about the following key areas that impact bank performance:

- Asset quality.
- Liquidity and interest rate risk positions.
- New products and services.
- Noninterest earnings.
- Off balance sheet items.
- Dividends.

2. Through discussions with the President, CEO, or Chairman, determine significant requests from the board for information to oversee business performance. Determine whether this information was incorporated into the board packet on a regular basis or if this was a one-time request.

3. Ascertain whether the board compares the bank's performance to that of its peers, and if so, how that information is used.

Objective: To determine that the board has accepted their responsibility for meeting the credit needs of all communities the bank serves.

1.   Discuss the bank's CRA efforts with the examiner assigned Community Reinvestment Act and the EIC. If a CRA exam is not being done concurrently, discuss the bank's efforts with the President or CEO and review the following information:

- Current CRA Public Evaluation
- Previous compliance Report of Examination
- Information contained in the OCC data base (i.e., community contacts, community group protests)

Objective: To assess compliance with laws, regulations, and prudent banking practice relating to duties and responsibilities of directors.

1.   Ascertain the bank's vulnerability to insider abuse and the level of compliance with established laws, regulations, and policies regarding insider transactions and activities.

Go to Insider Activities Examination Procedures.

2.   Ascertain whether the bank is in compliance with the following laws and regulations regarding **director qualifications**:

- Do all directors possess sufficient stock to qualify as directors? (12 U.S.C. 72, 12 CFR 7.2005)

- Are all directors citizens of the United States? (12 U.S.C. 72)
  - If not, has the Comptroller waived the citizenship requirement?

- Do a majority of the directors reside in the state, territory or district in which the bank is located, or within 100 miles of the bank's head office? (12 U.S.C. 72)

- Did a majority of the directors reside in the state, territory or district in which the bank is located, or within 100 miles of the bank's head office for 1 year prior to election? (12 U.S.C. 72)

- Did all directors take an oath of office? (12 U.S.C. 73 and 12 CFR 7.2008)

- Did the bank forward a copy of the oath of office to the OCC? (12 U.S.C. 73)

- Has the board ensured that no directors are engaged in the underwriting, sale or distribution of stocks, bonds or similar securities? (12 U.S.C. 78)
  - Has Federal Reserve Board approval been obtained for any that are? (12 U.S.C. 78)

- Have you determined that no director is an indenture trustee? (15 U.S.C. 77jjj)

3. Ascertain if the bank is in compliance with the following laws and regulations regarding **board structure**:

- Is the number of directors more than 5 and less than 25? (12 U.S.C. 71a)

- Did the board appoint directors to fill any vacancy? (12 U.S.C. 74)

- Did shareholders elect directors at their regular meeting? (12 U.S.C. 75)
  - If not, was the election held within 60 days thereof?

- Is the president a member of the board?(12 U.S.C. 76 and 12 CFR 7.2012)

- If necessary, has the bank notified the OCC of any new directors and senior officers? (12 U.S.C. 1831i)

4. Ascertain if the bank is in compliance with the following laws and regulations regarding **regulatory approvals**:

- Has the bank received written authorization from the FDIC for any director, officer or employee convicted of a crime involving a breach of trust or act of dishonesty? (12 U.S.C. 1829)

- Has the bank complied with provisions of any cease and desist agreement or order? (12 U.S.C. 1818(b))

- If the bank has any tie-ins of services, have they been approved as exceptions by the Federal Reserve Bank? (12 U.S.C. 1972)

- Has an officer of the bank made appropriate written reports when an embezzlement, misapplication, or similar transaction occurred? (12 CFR 21.11)

5. Ascertain compliance with the following laws and regulations regarding **regulatory reporting:**

- If embezzlements, defalcations, misappropriations, mysterious disappearances, or thefts have occurred since the previous examination, did the bank file a Suspicious Activity Report with the appropriate law enforcement agencies and with Treasury? (12 CFR 21.11)

- If the bank has more than 500 shareholders, did the bank publish reports in the form and with the content required under 12 CFR 11?

- Was the OCC notified of any change in control or change in CEO since the last examination? (12 U.S.C. 1817(j) and 12 CFR 5.50, 5.51)

- If the bank has any purchase money loans which are secured by 25 percent or more of the stock of a bank or savings and loan association has the appropriate federal regulator of that institution been notified? (12 U.S.C. 1817(j)(9))

- Does the bank maintain records of directors, executive officers, and principal shareholders and the related interest of those persons? (12 CFR 215)

- If the board contains honorary members, has the bank distinguished between honorary directors and active directors in published reports? (12 CFR 7.2004)

- Has the bank notified executive officers and principal shareholders of their reporting requirements (12 CFR 215)?

- Has the board held an organization meeting?

- Has a designated officer forwarded a list of directors to the OCC? (12 U.S.C. 73)

6. Ascertain compliance with the following laws and regulations regarding **restrictions on board activities:**

- Has a quorum been present for all board meetings? (12 CFR 7.2009)

- Do board procedures preclude any director from casting a vote by proxy? (12 CFR 7.2009)

- If there are any written employment contracts, are the terms reasonable? (12 CFR 30)

- If any management officials of the bank or its holding company or holding company affiliates are management officials of an unaffiliated depository institution or depository holding company, have the requirements of 12 U.S.C. 3201 and 12 CFR 26 been met?

- If any directors have been appointed to the board for purposes other than filling vacancies do the articles provide for such appointments? (12 CFR 7.2007)

7.   Determine compliance with the **Foreign Corrupt Practices Act** (15 U.S.C. 78dd-1 and 2) by:

- Reviewing the bank's policy prohibiting improper or illegal payments, bribes, kickbacks, etc., to any foreign government official or other person or organization covered by the law.

- Determining how that policy has been communicated to officers, employees or agents of the bank.

- Reviewing any investigation or study of the bank's policies and operations concerning the advance of funds in possible violation of the act done by, or on behalf of, the board of directors

- Discussing with the examiner assigned "Internal/External Audit" whether the internal/external auditors have established procedures to discover improper/illegal payments.

- Discussing with the examiner assigned "Internal Control" the general level of internal control to determine whether there is sufficient protection against improper/illegal payments being inaccurately recorded on the bank's books.

- Requesting examiners performing other programs to be alert for any transactions that might violate the provisions of the act.

- Compiling any information discovered throughout the examination on possible violations.

- Notifying the EIC and other appropriate OCC personnel of suspected criminal violations.

Objective: To assess compliance with administrative actions.

1. Determine compliance with administrative actions by reviewing:

   • Provisions of the document.
   • Bank records and performing necessary procedures to determine what the bank has done to comply and what remains to be done.

2. Prepare an Evaluation of Compliance with Formal or Informal Administrative Actions for inclusion in OCC data systems or the examination report, including:

   • Name of bank.
   • Nature of administrative action.
   • Date of administrative action.
   • Compliance with provisions of each article of the administrative action.
   • Nature and extent of noncompliance, including which articles were involved.
   • Action taken to ensure compliance where none exists.
   • Significant matters requiring attention that are not currently covered by the administrative action.
   • The effectiveness of the administrative action and whether additional administrative action should be taken or whether the administrative action should be terminated.
   • Determine compliance with any plan the OCC required to correct safety and soundness concerns (12 CFR 30.4).

Objective: Determine if corporate activities are consistent with organizational goals and fiduciary duties.

1. If it was not done in prior examinations, review and brief the by-laws and articles of association of the organization including:

   • Any specific provisions with respect to the requirements of directors.

   • The quorum requirements and if they were satisfied either according to recorded requirements or representation of more than one-half of the eligible shareholders (12 CFR 7.2009).

   If a brief exists from prior examinations, update it as appropriate. The resulting material should become a permanent part of the working papers and should be updated at subsequent examinations.

2. Read and brief the minutes of any stockholders' meetings. The brief should include a list of directors elected at the annual meeting, the number of shares present and voted, individuals acting as proxies, and specific action approved by shareholders.

3. Ascertain that all requirements were met (e.g., shareholder approval) for any of the following actions the board took since the last examination:

    - Any change of main office location outside the city limits (12 CFR 5.40).
    - Any issuance of preferred stock (12 CFR 5.46).
    - Any increase in capital stock, either through sale or through a stock dividend (12 CFR 5.46).
    - Any reduction in capital stock (12 CFR 5.46).
    - Any stock split (12 CFR 5.46).
    - Any bank pension plan established (see 29 U.S.C. 1001 regarding retirement accounts).
    - Any bank involvement in a conversion, merger, and/or consolidation (12 CFR 5.24).
    - All matters subject to vote at such meetings and assure that:
      - Cumulative voting is permitted at the election of directors only (12 U.S.C. 61, 12 CFR 7.2006).
      - Shares held by the bank as sole trustee or in its nominee name are not voted for directors (12 U.S.C. 61).
      - No officer, clerk, teller, or bookkeeper acted as a proxy (12 CFR 7.2002).
      - No shareholder whose liability was past-due was permitted to vote. Such liability is limited to that for stock subscription that is due and unpaid; no other liability is pertinent (12 U.S.C. 61).

4. Determine compliance with any conditions imposed in the approvals of corporate filings for:

    - Branches and relocation applications, including:
      - Capital plans or capital injections
      - Fixed asset limitations.
      - CRA plans.
    - Subordinated debt, operating subsidiaries, interim bank applications, including:
      - Capital plans.

      – Prior review and appropriate clearance of disclosures with the securities disclosure division.
- Mergers and acquisitions.

5.   Compare corporate activities to strategic objectives for compatibility. Consider:

- Expansion or shrinkage of company.
- Capital adequacy.
- Current and proposed business lines.
- Resources available (i.e., communication channels, delivery networks, managerial capacities and capabilities).

6.   Review the bank's practice of notifying shareholders of special or regular meetings. That notice must include the time, place, and purpose of the meeting. At least 10 days notice is required. Longer periods may be required by the articles of association, the by-laws, or other governing citations (12 U.S.C. 75, 12 CFR 7.2001).

7.   Determine the date of the annual shareholders' meeting, and that it was in compliance with the by-laws (12 U.S.C. 71).

8.   Review any stock option or stock purchase plan adopted since the preceding examination, and review such action for compliance with the articles of association and the various conditions of the articles of association.

9.   Determine if any candidate was nominated director, other than the slate nominated by bank management, and review for compliance with the requirements in 12 CFR 17.

Quality of Risk Management

Conclusion: The quality of risk management is (strong, satisfactory, weak)

Policy

Conclusion: The board (has, has not) established adequate policies to ensure compliance with laws and regulations applicable to the bank and its safety and soundness.

Objective: To ensure that the board has adopted policies that enable them to fulfill their duties and responsibilities as directors and to comply with laws and regulations relating to safety and soundness.

1.   Review policies specific to the board of directors, whether formal or informal, to determine whether they:

   - Are adequately reviewed/discussed and approved by the board of directors or delegated committee on an annual basis.
   - Establish effective guidelines for safety and soundness.
   - Provide flexibility to respond to changing conditions.

   Examples of common policies specific to the board of directors include:

   - Insider policies (required in writing by the OCC).
   - Management succession policies.
   - Compensation policies.

2.   Coordinate with the examination team the review of other policies governing the bank's operations.

3.   Through review of the board minutes or an update of previous work papers, identify those policies that have been formally approved by the board. Communicate this information to the examiners assigned those areas.

4.   Through discussion with management and other examiners, note any area of

---

banking activity for which policies should be developed.

Processes

Conclusion: Internal operating procedures, programs, and practices (are, are not) effective in enabling the board to comply with laws and regulations and to ensure the safety and soundness of the bank.

Objective: To ensure that bank operating procedures, programs, and practices are adequate to enable the board to fulfill their duties and responsibilities.

1.   Determine whether a process exists to enable the board to remain informed of the bank's legal and regulatory framework. Consider director participation in:

   - Management presentations on bank activities and developments in the industry.
   - Bank counsel briefings or reports on legislative and regulatory changes, pending litigation, and emerging compliance issues or other legal developments.
   - External outreach and training sessions by industry organizations and regulatory agencies.

2.   Determine the board's involvement in the bank's planning process.

   - Is the board active in the development of the bank's vision?
   - Does the board reassess the plan periodically to consider new opportunities or to respond to unanticipated external developments?
   - Does the board review and approve any proposed departures from the long- and short-term business plans of the bank before they take place?

3.   Through discussions with the examination team, determine whether effective procedures, programs, and practices exist to promote the safety and soundness of the bank. Discuss with the examiners reviewing other areas of the bank any deficiencies they have discovered.

4.   Determine the mechanism used to assign responsibility for correcting deficiencies noted in regulatory reports, internal audit reports, external

audit reports or any other reports to the board, and the board's system of determining compliance.

5.   Ascertain if the bank is in compliance with the following laws and regulations regarding internal controls:

- Does the bank ensure that they make no loans to national bank examiners? (18 U.S.C. 212 and 213)
- Did you ensure that the bank has not made any political contributions? (2 U.S.C. 441b)
- Does the bank have a system to ensure that no employees have misappropriated funds, made false entries, or otherwise defrauded the bank? (18 U.S.C. 656)
- Does the bank have a system to ensure that no extortionate extensions of credit occur? (18 U.S.C. 892, 893, and 894)
- Does the bank have a process to ensure that no checks are certified against uncollected funds? (18 U.S.C. 1004)
- Does the bank have a process to ensure that no unauthorized obligations of the bank are issued? (18 U.S.C. 1005 and 1006)

6.   Determine how directors perform a director's examination, the frequency of such examinations, and what part the directors take in the process.

7.   Check the last report of examination that was returned to the bank to determine that it was signed by the members of the board or an authorized committee thereof.

Personnel

Conclusion: The board (is, is not) aware of their duties and responsibilities.

Objective: To ensure that the board members are aware of their duties and fiduciary responsibilities and are capable of fulfilling them.

1.   Determine through review of board minutes and through discussions with the EIC whether the directors are knowledgeable of their duties and responsibilities.

- Refer to The Directors Book outlining the duties and responsibilities of directors.

2. Review previous board actions to determine responsiveness of directors in implementing necessary corrective action.

- Prior examination report findings.
- Bank correspondence indicating board actions.
- The accuracy and timeliness of regulatory reports.

Controls

Conclusion: Control systems and information systems (are, are not) effective to ensure compliance with regulatory requirements regarding the duties and responsibilities of directors.

Objective: To ensure that the board has established effective internal controls and information systems that enable them to comply with laws and regulations relating to their duties and responsibilities.

1. Review the internal and external audit functions as they relate to duties and responsibilities of directors.

- Do they review insider transactions for compliance with laws, rulings, and regulations?
- Does the board take timely corrective action to address deficiencies noted by the audit, compliance, and/or internal loan functions so that the procedures, programs, and practices are adequate to assist the board in discharging their duties and responsibilities?

2. Determine whether information systems used by the board to measure bank performance, make decisions, and assess effectiveness of existing policies/procedures are adequate.

- Are bank information systems considered effective in providing timely and accurate information for board use?
- Are board appointed committees effective in facilitating bank operations?
- Do the systems generate adequate information so that the board is

aware of any problems in the bank as they are developing?

Conclusion

Objective: Prepare written conclusion comments and communicate findings to management/board.

1. Provide EIC with conclusions of findings.

    - Overall conclusions.
    - Recommendations.
    - Violations of law and regulation.

2. Determine the impact on the aggregate and direction of risk assessments for any applicable risks identified by performing the above procedures. Examiners should refer to guidance provided under the OCC's large and community bank risk assessment programs.

    - Risk Categories: Compliance, Credit, Foreign Currency Translation, Interest Rate, Liquidity, Price, Reputation, Strategic, Transaction
    - Risk Conclusions: High, Moderate, or Low
    - Risk Direction: Increasing, Stable, or Decreasing

3. Determine in consultation with the EIC, if the risks identified are significant enough to merit bringing them to the board's attention in the report of examination. If so, prepare items for inclusion under the heading Matters Requiring Board Attention (MRBA).

    - MRBA should cover practices that:
      - Deviate from sound fundamental principles and are likely to result in financial deterioration if not addressed.
      - Result in substantive noncompliance with laws.
    - MRBA should discuss:
      - Causative factors contributing to the problem.
      - Consequences of inaction.
      - Management's commitment for corrective action.
      - The time frame and person(s) responsible for corrective action.

4. Discuss findings with management/board including conclusions

---

regarding applicable risks.

- Overall conclusions.
- Recommendations.
- Violations of law or regulation.
- Deficiencies.
- If applicable, obtain commitments from management and confirmation of those commitments from the board to correct violations of law and/or Matters Requiring Board Attention.

5. As appropriate, prepare comments for inclusion in the report of examination.

6. Prepare a memorandum or update the work program with any information that will facilitate future examinations.

7. Update OCC's electronic information system and any applicable report of examination schedules or tables.

8. Organize and reference working papers in accordance with OCC guidelines.